Transcending Race in America
Biographies of Biracial Achievers

Halle Berry

Beyoncé

David Blaine

Mariah Carey

Frederick Douglass

W. E. B. Du Bois

Salma Hayek

Derek Jeter

Alicia Keys

Soledad O'Brien

Rosa Parks

Prince

Booker T. Washington

MARIAH CAREY

Singer, Songwriter, Record Producer, and Actress

Kerrily Sapet

Mason Crest Publishers

Produced by 21st Century Publishing and Communications, Inc.

MASON CREST PUBLISHERS INC.
370 Reed Road
Broomall, Pennsylvania 19008
(866) MCP-BOOK (toll free)
www.masoncrest.com

Printed in the United States of America.

First Printing

9 8 7 6 5 4 3 2 1

Library of Congress Cataloging-in-Publication Data

Sapet, Kerrily, 1972–
    Mariah Carey : singer, songwriter, record producer, actress / Kerrily Sapet.
        p. cm. — (Transcending race in America : biographies of biracial achievers)
    Includes bibliographical references (p.) and index.
    ISBN 978-1-4222-1613-2 (hardback : alk. paper) — ISBN 978-1-4222-1627-9 (pbk. : alk. paper)
    1. Carey, Mariah—Juvenile literature. 2. Singers—United States—Biography—Juvenile
literature. I. Title.
ML3930.C257S27 2010
782.42164092—dc22
[B]   2009022044

Publisher's notes:
All quotations in this book come from original sources, and contain the spelling and grammatical inconsistencies of the original text.

The Web sites mentioned in this book were active at the time of publication. The publisher is not responsible for Web sites that have changed their addresses or discontinued operation since the date of publication. The publisher will review and update the Web site addresses each time the book is reprinted.

Table of Contents

> " I HAVE BROTHERS, SISTERS, NIECES,
> NEPHEWS, UNCLES, AND COUSINS,
> OF EVERY RACE AND EVERY HUE,
> SCATTERED ACROSS THREE CONTINENTS,
> AND FOR AS LONG AS I LIVE,
> I WILL NEVER FORGET THAT
> IN NO OTHER COUNTRY ON EARTH
> IS MY STORY EVEN POSSIBLE. "

> " WE MAY HAVE DIFFERENT STORIES,
> BUT WE HOLD COMMON HOPES. . . .
> WE MAY NOT LOOK THE SAME
> AND WE MAY NOT HAVE
> COME FROM THE SAME PLACE,
> BUT WE ALL WANT TO MOVE
> IN THE SAME DIRECTION —
> TOWARDS A BETTER FUTURE . . . "

— BARACK OBAMA, 44TH PRESIDENT
OF THE UNITED STATES OF AMERICA

AMERICA'S SUPERSTAR

MARIAH CAREY'S WORLD ROCKED. PEOPLE loved her extraordinary singing voice, whether whispering soft or storming loud. In April 2008, she scored her 18th number-one hit. She had more chart-topping **singles** than any solo artist in America, even Elvis Presley. Only the legendary Beatles, with their world record of 20 number-one hits, stood in her way.

Mariah crashed onto the music scene nearly 20 years ago with her best-selling self-titled album. Her first five singles rocketed to the top of the U.S. *Billboard* Hot 100 list, something no other recording artist had done. Soon she had spent more weeks at the number-one spot on the charts than anyone else, including The Beatles. When reporters asked her about challenging their record number of hits, she said,

Mariah Carey beams with joy on receiving a Special Achievement Award at the 2008 World Music Awards. Mariah's star had risen like a rocket over the past 20 years, and she found herself at the height of musical and personal success she had barely dreamed of as a child.

"I really can never put myself in the category of people who have not only revolutionized music, but also changed the world. That's a completely different era and time. . . . I'm just feeling really happy and grateful."

AWESOME ACHIEVEMENTS

Mariah's first album kick-started her career. Since then she has racked up at least 150 awards for her music. Across different categories of music, singers can win awards for songs, albums,

The Beatles have a world record 20 number-one hits, but Mariah is close behind with 18. Mariah is modest about her superstardom, not wanting to put herself in the same category as those legendary musicians. She says she is just grateful to be where she is today.

Beatle Mania

Calling themselves The Beatles, four teenagers from England burst onto the music scene in the 1960s. Paul McCartney, Ringo Starr, George Harrison, and John Lennon would make The Beatles one of history's greatest rock and roll groups. In 1964, they appeared on a popular American television program, *The Ed Sullivan Show*. More than 70 million viewers, young and old, watched them perform. Soon everyone was singing their songs and calling them The Fab Four.

With their energetic singing and catchy melodies, The Beatles started a music revolution. They are "the greatest composers since Beethoven," wrote one music critic. Crazed crowds mobbed the stars. At concerts, girls fainted from excitement at the sound of their voices and their charming good looks. Fans bought Beatles albums, clothes, posters, and even lunchboxes.

Twenty of their songs became number-one hits in the U.S., such as "I Want to Hold Your Hand," "Yesterday," and "All You Need is Love." Although The Beatles broke up and their music changed, their fans stayed loyal. As of 2009, The Beatles had sold more than one billion albums worldwide. For many years no one has come close to breaking their record 20 chart-topping hits, except Mariah.

and performances. Sometimes one album has won Mariah three prizes: one for the album, one for an individual song, and one for the way she sang it.

Receiving a **Grammy Award**, American Music Award, Billboard Award, or a World Music Award is a great honor for a singer. Although there are many different awards, these four are considered the most prestigious. Many singers dream of winning even one. Mariah has won an impressive total of 5 Grammy Awards, 10 American Music Awards, 19 World Music Awards, and 19 Billboard Awards. She also has received honors for setting new records and selling incredible numbers of albums.

For many years, fans have voted her their favorite female artist of the year. Mariah has also won awards for donating time and money to charity. Many groups, and even a U.S. president, have recognized her generosity.

Mariah's record-breaking achievements are a wish come true. She always dreamed of becoming a famous singer and sharing her music with the world. Over the years, many people were prejudiced against her because she is biracial. Mariah, who is part Irish, African American, and Venezuelan, said, "I'm happy with the combination of things I am." Mariah has overcome their unkind behavior and cruelty to become a stunning success. She told reporters,

> **"For me, in my mind the accomplishment is just that much sweeter. In terms of my ethnicity, always feeling like an outsider, always feeling different . . . for me it's about saying, 'Thank you Lord, for giving me the faith to believe in myself when other people had written me off.'"**

Amazing Ability

Mariah could sing names and numbers from the phone book and sound incredible, said one music critic. Her voice has impressed critics, fans, and other musicians. Mariah's **range** and power are greater than those of many other singers. In 2003, the *Guinness Book of World Records* listed her as singing the highest note hit by a human voice. Producer Jimmy Jam said,

> **"I can't even think that high. It's not that she can hit the notes. A lot of people hit the notes. But the runs and trills that people do in a normal register she does at the top of her voice."**

While many singers are known for one style, Mariah likes to experiment with different types of music. She fills her albums with a variety of songs, some inspired by the music she heard as a young girl, and others by cutting-edge sounds. She often works with other famous singers and musicians, using new ideas and sounds to keep her songs fresh. Her soft, slow, romantic **ballads** are the songs that first won her fame. Since then she has produced dance hits with fast beats and songs with **hip-hop** rhythms.

Mariah's music can be bouncy, light, and playful. It can also be slow, serious, and packed with emotion. Mariah writes the words

Mariah shows off her amazing vocal style at the Grammy Nominations Concert Live! in December 2008. Her power and awesome voice range are showcased in her many award-winning albums, which Mariah fills with her own songs and a variety of musical styles that delight fans worldwide.

to her own songs, which is unusual. Her songs sometimes tell the story of her life. Often they are about relationships. Many of her fans identify with the experiences she includes in her lyrics. Her songs put their emotions—love, happiness, sorrow, or even anger—to music. Music has long been Mariah's love, helping her through good and bad times. She says,

Mariah greets fans welcoming her tour to London, England. Her music—from ballads to hip-hop—appeals to so many different types of people that sell-out crowds attend her concerts all over the world. Fans at home and abroad have eagerly bought more than 200 million of Mariah's albums.

"I use everything I've ever thought about in my songs. And whatever the melody makes me feel is what I gear the lyrics towards."

WORLD FAME

Fans around the world—from the United States to Africa to Europe to Asia—have snapped up more than 200 million of her albums. When Mariah has gone on tour, thousands of people have attended her concerts. Although the shows are held in huge arenas, often tickets sell out at record speeds.

Millions of people watch when Mariah performs on television shows or appears in videos. She has been featured in newspapers, magazines, and advertisements around the world. Across the Internet, many fan clubs and Web sites are dedicated to Mariah. Fans chat and E-mail about the latest events in her life or her music. Their excitement ramps up when Mariah gets ready to release a new song. Nearly 300,000 people downloaded "Touch My Body," her latest chart topper, in its first week, setting another new record.

With her ability and style, Mariah's music appeals to many types of people. Her fans have their favorites among her 18 number-one singles. Some people love her ballads "Hero" and "Vision of Love." Others prefer her hip-hop hits like "So Lonely" and "Honey."

Singing has earned Mariah millions of dollars and made her world famous. It also has given her the opportunity to make a difference to others in the world. With her money and fame, she tries to help children and families in need. Mariah also concentrates on doing what she loves—singing. She states,

"Music is what I love and it's what I feel. . . . [To] know that I can do something that I enjoy and hopefully bring some enjoyment to other people through what I do is an incredible feeling and I'm just really thankful for it."

Chapter

2

❧ ❀ ❧

A
LONELY
GIRL

MARIAH CAREY NEEDED A SECRET DREAM.
People often treated her cruelly because her family
looked different. Her mother, Patricia, was Irish,
and her father, Alfred, was African American and
Venezuelan. As a young girl Mariah imagined music
as her ticket out of her rough neighborhood, and
singing helped her believe in herself.

Mariah was born on March 27, 1970, in Long Island, New
York. Her parents named her after a song, "They Call the Wind
Mariah." From the moment her parents married, they had
faced **racism**. Patricia's family disowned her because Alfred was
black. Although the **civil rights movement** made laws fairer
for African Americans, attitudes changed slowly. Mariah told
People magazine,

As a biracial girl, Mariah dreamed of escaping the discrimination her family had faced as she grew up in rough neighborhoods. Music helped her deal with her loneliness. Mariah's early-blooming talent made her feel good about herself and inspired her to keep trying to break into show business.

"They went through some very hard times before I was born. They had their dogs poisoned, their cars set on fire and blown up. It put a strain on their relationship. There was always this tension. They just fought all the time."

Mariah and her older brother and sister, Morgan and Allison, didn't fit in either. Because they were biracial, neighborhood bullies teased them and picked fights. The pressure on Mariah's parents became too much. They divorced when she was young, splitting up the family.

AGAINST THE WORLD

After the divorce, Mariah's mother, an opera singer, had to work several jobs. They had little money and moved around a lot. Sometimes they slept on a friend's floor because they had no place else to go.

Mariah had to grow up fast. Her mother often left her home alone while she was at work. Mariah was lonely, and music became her friend. She recalled,

> **"My mother would have to tear me away from the radio every night just to get me to go to bed. But then I would sneak back down to the kitchen, bring the radio back into my bedroom, and listen to it under the covers. I used to sing myself to sleep every night."**

One day, Mariah's mother heard her singing an opera song in Italian. She recognized her daughter's amazing talent and began giving Mariah voice lessons.

BORN TO SING

Mariah quickly soaked up music. She sang constantly. She said, "I'd mimic whatever I heard, whether it was my brother's or sister's records, or whatever songs were on the radio at the time."

Mariah loved **soul** singers like and Aretha Franklin and James Brown, the swinging sounds of jazz and **R&B**. She especially liked Minnie Riperton, who could hit notes few other singers could dream of hitting. Mariah also listened to **gospel** music and songs from the streets.

Mariah knew she wanted to be a singer, even when people tried to stop her. She told *Rolling Stone* magazine,

"I loved singing. I was singing since I started talking. . . . So I was singing at the [dinner] table . . . and my father said, 'There will be no singing at the table!' So I got up from the table, and I went into the living room, and I got on the coffee table and continued singing at the top of my lungs."

Mariah liked to sing to herself and write poems in her journal, combining them in her head. Most singers don't write their own lyrics. Mariah and Alicia Keys, another biracial recording artist, are among the few who can.

Among Mariah's early influences was soul singer James Brown. She also loved jazz, rhythm and blues, and gospel music. No matter what musical style she was soaking up at the time, she performed at home at the top of her lungs, even when no one wanted to listen!

Mariah hung out at recording studios in her teens, first as a backup singer and then creating her own demo tape. When she moved to Manhattan, she was determined to follow her dream. Sure enough, her extraordinary talent was noticed and she soon signed a recording contract.

Musical Keys

Alicia Keys's soft, soulful voice has won dozens of prestigious awards and sold millions of albums. Alicia grew up in New York City and has also starred in movies like *The Nanny Diaries*. Alicia is part Irish, part Italian, and part Jamaican. Like Mariah, Alicia too has overcome racism. She said,

66 Even when you feel that nobody else feels what you're going through and all you see is negative, just keep on keeping on . . . [and] you can be whatever you wanna be, you just have to believe it. Say this is who I am, and you will grow into the person you want to become. 99

CHASING HER DREAM

When Mariah was 14 years old, she landed a job as a backup singer, often working at the recording studio until dawn. Her friends nicknamed her "Mirage" because she was often absent from school. Her grades suffered, but Mariah just wanted to sing. She said,

66 Because my mom sang for a living, I knew it could be more than a pipe dream. My mom always told me 'You are special. You have talent.' From a very early age, she gave me the belief that I could do this. 99

On Mariah's 16th birthday, her brother gave her money to make a demo tape, to show producers her ability. When she graduated from high school, she packed up her belongings and demo tape. She moved to Manhattan, hoping to break into music.

Mariah worked several jobs. Money was tight, and she survived on pasta and bagels. She tried to get record companies to listen to her tape. She remembered it as "a year of crying yourself to sleep at night because you want to do something so badly."

One night at a party, Mariah had the chance to pass her demo tape to Tommy Mottola, head of Sony Music Entertainment. When Mottola listened to her tape, he said she was "destined for stardom." Soon Mariah signed a record contract and began working on her first album.

LIVING THE DREAM

PEOPLE LIKED WHAT THEY HEARD AND SAW when Mariah performed. Not only did she have a stunning voice, but she was also tall and attractive, with long, honey-blond curls. She worked hard to make her album perfect. Mariah's **debut** album launched a decade of success, making her one of the most famous singers in the world.

In 1990, Mariah released her album, *Mariah Carey*. The album shot up to the number-one spot on the *Billboard* charts. It stayed there for 22 weeks. *Mariah Carey* became the best-selling album in the United States. It sold 12 million copies and went **platinum**.

The songs Mariah picked for her first album showed off the range and power of her voice. When one producer heard her sing, he got goose bumps. A reporter wrote,

Mariah can't stop smiling as she holds her 1991 Grammy Awards for Best New Artist and Best Female Pop Vocal Performance. Her first album launched her to stardom as it debuted at number one on the charts and stayed there for almost six months. Mariah's dream was turning into reality.

> "This is a voice that can probably shatter glass and put it back together, that sounds as if she's taking the words and twirling them over her head like a cowboy with a lasso."

THE WORLD MEETS MARIAH

The music and lyrics on *Mariah Carey* were personal. The soul, jazz, and gospel music she listened to as a young girl had inspired her. She told *Ebony* magazine the number-one hit "Vision of

Love," "represents everything in my life. It is a song from the heart." Soon "Love Takes Time" also topped the charts.

At the Grammy Awards, Mariah performed in front of millions of TV viewers. She won two Grammys, one for best new artist and another for her performance of "Vision of Love." A month later, at the Soul Train Awards, she won awards for best new artist, single, and album.

Soon "Love Takes Time" was named the top song of the year. Readers of *Rolling Stone* magazine voted her the best new singer. With her first album, Mariah had achieved more than most singers do in a lifetime.

FAME AND FORTUNE

Fame came fast. Suddenly photographers snapped pictures wherever Mariah went. Newspaper and magazine reporters clamored for interviews. Television hosts wanted her to appear on shows.

Mariah now could buy the things she had wanted as a young girl. She bought clothes and a fancy convertible. She moved into an apartment with a beautiful view of New York City. The fame was fun, but she told *Parade* magazine,

> **"I don't do it just because I want to make money or I want to be famous. I need to make music. If I didn't have this, I don't know where I would be."**

Many people wondered whether Mariah was black or white. Some people accused her of trying to sound like black singers. She said, "I'm very ambiguous looking. I could be anything, really." Mariah had dealt with racism her entire life. She told reporters from *Ebony* magazine,

> **"Some people look at me and they see my light skin and my hair. I can't help the way I look . . . I don't try to look a certain way or sing a certain way. . . . And if people enjoy my music, then they shouldn't care what I am, so it shouldn't be an issue."**

In the end, Mariah's music won. Most people forgot about the color of her skin. They just listened to her beautiful voice.

TOPPING THE CHARTS

Mariah kept working hard. She spent long hours making videos and planning her next album. Mariah teamed up with other musicians and writers to give this album a different flavor, with more gospel and soul sounds. *Emotions* debuted in 1991. It topped the charts, proving Mariah wasn't just a one-time hit. Fans bought

Mariah enjoys rehearsing with actor Patrick Swayze on the set of *Saturday Night Live* in 1991. Suddenly she was famous and in demand—for television appearances, interviews, and photo shoots. Although Mariah could now buy anything she wanted, she kept focusing on her music, which was more important than her new wealth.

Mariah's 1991 album, *Emotions*, was another smash, offering fans more gospel and soul music. The record raced to the top of the charts, and three singles were number-one hits. Mariah is the only musician whose first five singles all reached number one.

A Role Model

Famous golfer Tiger Woods calls himself "Cablinasian"—a mix of Caucasian, black, American Indian, and Asian. His popularity, along with that of other biracial stars like Mariah, is changing attitudes. For years people have treated biracial individuals unfairly. Mariah told *Parade* magazine,

❝I felt very much like an outcast when I was younger. No matter where I went, there was always this sense of not really falling into one place or into one category. I moved around a lot when I was growing up, so nobody knew me and I was never one thing or another. Being biracial, I didn't really have somebody to look at and say, 'Okay, this person is exactly the same as me, and they're out there.' A lot of kids have said that to me, 'Until you put your first record out, I didn't feel like there was anybody the same as me.' People who don't feel like they fit in can identify with me.❞

Today, biracial children have role models in entertainment, education, and sports. More families are mixes of different races, cultures, and religions. An estimated 7.2 million Americans are biracial. Although racism still exists, more people look beyond the color of someone's skin.

three million copies of the album. Her songs "Emotions," "I Don't Wanna Cry," and "Someday" became number-one hits. Mariah was the only artist to have her first five singles reach number one on the charts.

For all Mariah's success, she still feared performing live. In the recording studio she could make mistakes and correct them. She couldn't do that live. She told *USA Today*,

❝Touring is hard for me because I'm not a ham. You have to be dynamic and showy, and that's not second nature to me. I didn't get a chance to work my way up from the clubs, so performing is still pretty scary.❞

Nevertheless, Mariah agreed to a performance on MTV *Unplugged*. Her show was so popular that MTV aired it over and over. She made an album from the show, donating some of the money to charity.

DREAMS COME TRUE

For months people wondered if she and Tommy Mottola were dating. The two had fallen in love, but they kept their relationship a secret. Some people said he made Mariah a star because he loved her. Mariah responded, "Somebody as powerful as Tommy can help people get started, but they can't make people sell millions of records."

Soon their secret was out. Mariah had been a poor, hard-working beauty who met a charming, powerful prince. "It really is like Cinderella," she said.

They married on June 5, 1993, in a fairy-tale wedding. Mariah wore a long white gown and 47 girls tossed flower petals. Other famous singers, like Bruce Springsteen and Ozzy Osbourne, helped them celebrate.

The Starmaker

Tommy Mottola grew up acting and singing. When his first album wasn't a hit, he turned to the business side of music. He worked hard to become one of the music industry's most powerful men.

Tommy Mottola proved to be a very good judge of talent. Soon he was handling the careers of superstars like John Mellencamp and Carly Simon. In 1988, Tommy Mottola moved to Sony Music Entertainment, and signed stars like Mariah, Jennifer Lopez, and Pearl Jam to the label.

Tommy Mottola is famous for his lavish lifestyle. He lives in homes worth millions of dollars, and drives expensive cars. After he and Mariah divorced, Tommy Mottola remarried and started his own entertainment company, Casablanca Records.

BUSY YEARS

Soon Mariah released another album, *Music Box*. It topped the charts for eight weeks, and went platinum. Two singles from the album, "Dreamlover" and "Hero," became number-one hits.

Mariah also went on tour, although performing was tough on her voice. Her first shows were rough, but soon her confidence grew. Mariah received Billboard and American Music Awards for top album, top artist, and favorite artist.

Mariah proudly shows off the platinum status of several of her albums. During her busy early years, it seemed as if every record she released turned to gold—or platinum—and led to numerous awards. She clearly was becoming a new force in the music industry.

Mariah continued releasing albums with huge success. In 1994, she released an album of Christmas songs, and then the album *Daydream.* She also went on a world tour. In 1996, she took home two American Music Awards, four Billboard Awards, and four World Music Awards.

Mariah attends a Police Athletic League (PAL) fundraiser in New York City with husband Tommy Mottola, who had managed her early career before they married in 1993. Mariah has always worked with organizations like PAL and the Fresh Air Fund to help needy children have better lives.

HELPING OTHERS

Mariah's sister had a difficult life. Before she was 20 years old, she had become pregnant, started using drugs, and contracted **AIDS**. Mariah had escaped the same path by holding onto her dream. "You could be anything you wanted to be when you had music," she said. Mariah wanted to help children make better choices than her sister had. She said,

> **"When I found out she had AIDS I cried for days. She could never really care for her son again. . . . This sad family story made me care more about other children in need. To give them advice and to see that they get a better life. . . . Some kids just don't have a role model in their lives, someone they can get comfort from, to point out the right direction in their lives."**

Mariah worked with the Police Athletic League in New York City, providing opportunities for inner-city children to explore creative arts. She helped raise money and played basketball with the children.

Mariah also helped the Fresh Air Fund, offering children from tough neighborhoods a chance to go to summer camp. She donated one million dollars. She visited the camp, named Camp Mariah, and had foot races with the campers.

THE FAIRY TALE ENDS

Although Mariah's career was successful, her marriage was falling apart. People gossiped about their relationship. Now used to fame, Mariah said, "You have to expect people to talk about you . . . and there are a lot worse things they could say."

Mariah had grown tired of her husband controlling her career. He listened in on her phone conversations and had bodyguards following her. Before long, she and Tommy Mottola divorced.

Mariah soon met Derek Jeter, the popular New York Yankees shortstop. Jeter was also biracial. They dated for a short time. After they split up, Mariah began seeing Luis Miguel, a popular Latino singer.

A NEW LOOK

After her divorce Mariah began to express herself more. She changed her image, beginning to wear more glamorous, sexier outfits. She wanted her music to be different too, with more hip-hop on her next album, *Butterfly*.

Mariah began to work with artists like Q-Tip and Missy (Misdemeanor) Elliott, who said Mariah's "straight up. She's cool. She's rap." Mariah and Sean "Diddy" Combs worked together on the song "Honey," which quickly became a number-one hit. Fans bought the album by the millions. Mariah was right about her new hip-hop style. She said,

> **"I grew up listening to it. . . . I started with the Sugarhill Gang. I know and respect what hip-hop artists do . . . [The new album] was a turning point for me because it was an official street record. I'd be walking around New York and hear it blasting out of Jeeps."**

Mariah was busy. She launched another world tour and tried to help new artists. She said, "I know exactly how it feels to have a tape and not to have anybody listening to it seriously." In 1998 Mariah racked up more awards: an American Music Award, a Billboard Award, and two World Music Awards.

NEW PROJECTS

In 1999, Mariah released her eighth album, *Rainbow*. It gave her another chart-topping hit, "Heartbreaker," which she performed with rapper Jay-Z. Mariah was ready to add on to her singing career.

Mariah wanted to work as an actress, too. She took acting lessons and worked on soundtracks for several movies, such as *Men in Black*. For the movie *The Prince of Egypt*, she sang "When You Believe" with Whitney Houston.

Mariah and Whitney Houston were rumored to be rivals. However, they quickly became friends. After performing the song at the 1999 Academy Awards show, they won an Oscar for the Best Original Song.

Mariah and music legend Whitney Houston combine their soulful voices, singing "When You Believe" at the 1999 Academy Awards ceremony. By the end of the 1990s Mariah's success was legendary. Eight of her albums had topped the charts, and she had won almost every award the music industry could offer.

A Music Legend

Whitney Houston was destined to sing. In 1983, a producer heard her singing at a nightclub and signed her on the spot. Her first album, *Whitney Houston*, became a best seller, launching seven number-one hits, like "The Greatest Love of All." Her song "I Will Always Love You" became the biggest-selling single in history.

Whitney Houston is famous for her rhythmic ballads. She was one of the first African-American female artists to receive much coverage on MTV. Many young singers today have been influenced by her.

Singing sensation Whitney Houston has sold more than 170 million albums, singles, and videos, and won 6 Grammys and 23 American Music Awards. She has starred in movies and produced shows, like *The Cheetah Girls*. She is well known for her charity work.

Mariah beams as she is honored for her efforts on behalf of young adults at the Congressional Awards Gala in 1999. Few celebrities have done as much as Mariah has to raise money to help needy children, and to spend time with them in meaningful ways.

AT THE TOP

The 1990s were a blur of success for Mariah. She received the most prestigious awards in the music world. Eight of her albums topped the charts, and they were sold in millions. She had 14 number-one hit songs, and broke The Beatles' record for spending the most weeks at the top spot on the charts.

Mariah also learned to deal with her fame and fortune. She took control of her personal and public life. In 1999, when Mariah accepted a Billboard Award for Artist of the Decade, she said,

> **"I owe this to the fans and I will never forget you, so I want to accept this award on behalf of all of you. We've come a long way and I feel like I'm just getting started. Because as an artist, and most importantly as a person, I am genuinely happy to finally be free to be who I am."**

Although Mariah realized her dream, she remembered others who were less fortunate. To help countless children, she raised money, held charity benefits, and donated her time. One Christmas she took 100 needy children on a vacation. They rode sleds, sang, and decorated gingerbread houses. In 1999, she received a Congressional Award, honoring her volunteer work.

With such success in the early years of her career, many wondered what Mariah would accomplish next. However, the years ahead would be difficult. They would test her belief in herself and her abilities.

Chapter

4

TOUGH TIMES

MARIAH HAD 10 YEARS OF INCREDIBLE success. At the World Music Awards in 2000, one billion TV viewers watched her accept the Bestselling Female Artist of the Millennium award for selling more albums than any other female artist. However, in the following years, she struggled.

Mariah worked constantly and slept little. Producer Jimmy Jam observed,

> **"She works really hard. . . . She doesn't have to prove herself, but she feels like she does. [Once] . . . she worked all night and left the studio at 7:00 in the morning. Four hours later she was shooting a video. She shoots the video all day, goes to dinner . . . comes back to the studio and records all night until 7:00 the following morning."**

Mariah relaxes with kids from New York City at her Fresh Air Camp in 2000. Her many volunteer activities kept Mariah busy, along with her hectic recording and performing schedule. The stress proved too much for her, and she had to take time off from her career.

Volunteer work also occupied Mariah's time. At the VH1 Divas Show she and other famous singers helped raise money for the Save the Music Foundation, which supports school music programs. At the benefit, Mariah achieved her dream of performing with Diana Ross, a childhood idol.

TOO MUCH, TOO FAST

Mariah continued her dream of acting, too. She was putting together a soundtrack for the movie *Glitter*. She also had a starring

A Supreme Star

African-American singer Diana Ross grew up in the some of the poorest neighborhoods of Detroit, Michigan. By the young age of 15 she was leading The Supremes to their 12 number-one hits, like "Someday We'll Be Together" and "You Can't Hurry Love." In 1969 she went solo, becoming the first female solo artist with six number-one hits.

Diana Ross is known for combining soul, R&B, jazz, and Motown. She has performed on television, in movies, and in Broadway shows, selling more than 100 million albums. She has inspired young stars, like the Jackson 5.

In 2007 President George W. Bush presented her with a lifetime achievement award. Diana Ross has entertained fans for more than 50 years. She is still singing strong.

role, and spent long hours on the movie set. *Glitter* told the story of a young girl who became a world-famous star overnight. Mariah went on a 14-day tour to publicize the movie. The stress began to take its toll.

To make matters worse, Mariah and Sony were disagreeing about the style of her songs. Her relationship with Sony had been difficult since her divorce. She called it "a complete mess." Soon she broke with Sony.

Mariah signed a contract with Virgin Records for $80 million, the biggest recording contract in history. She told reporters, "Jobs change, and people change positions. I am looking forward to recording a new album, and making a new movie."

BREAKDOWN

Mariah's movie and soundtrack flopped. Making the disappointment worse, her relationship with Luis Miguel fizzled. Unhappy and tired, Mariah began to behave strangely. She appeared on an MTV show wearing a T-shirt over short shorts and handing out popsicles. She told VH1,

"I'm honestly really, really delirious and stressed out and overworked and doing too much. . . . It's an insane time in my life. It's crazy. Everything is going on like really fast."

Mariah's family and friends grew increasingly concerned. She started leaving strange messages on her Web site. She told fans, "I really don't feel that I should be doing music right now."

At the end of July, Mariah suffered an emotional and physical breakdown. She checked into a psychiatric hospital. Rumors flew.

Mariah moved into the film world with an acting role and soundtrack for the movie *Glitter*. Neither was a success, and her break with Sony Records made life difficult as well. The endless hours of work had completely worn Mariah down.

Mariah happily returns to the spotlight, announcing that she would sing the national anthem at Super Bowl XXXVI in 2002. She showed the world she was back on her feet as she started work on a new album and also returned to acting.

People suggested Mariah was depressed, suicidal, and even insane. Virgin Records paid Mariah to break her contract early. Many people said Mariah's career was over.

In the Spotlight

Fancy limousines, mansions, expensive clothes, piles of money, and all the attention you could want. What could be better? Most stars agree that being famous is fun. But life in the spotlight isn't always easy.

Big celebrities have little privacy. Often fans and reporters want to know every detail of their lives—from their latest relationship to their favorite ice cream flavor. Some stars have trouble taking walks or eating in restaurants without fans asking for autographs. Sometimes fans get dangerously close, even invading stars' homes.

With cameras constantly snapping, people see the good, the bad, and the ugly in a celebrity's life. It's hard to make a mistake without the world knowing. Still, most people would choose to be famous.

BACK ON HER FEET

Mariah forced herself to return to the public's eye. In 2002, she sang at the Super Bowl, her first public appearance in months. Mariah inked a fresh contract, for $23 million, with Island Def Jam. She began working on another album, *Charmbracelet*. She appeared on the TV show *The View*, performing the song "I Only Wanted" from her new album. She told listeners,

"The album is kind of like a hopeful celebration of life. During that celebration, we have the ups and the downs, and the different songs."

The music on Mariah's album told of her troubles. Her song and video, "Through the Rain" symbolized her life. She struggled through the rain, the tough times, to succeed. Critics gave the album mixed reviews. One said, "She has to make her fans forget a movie they probably didn't see and an album they probably didn't buy."

Mariah's fans related to the difficulties in her life. One fan wrote to her,

"**I can identify with you even more now, because you're human. I just feel like its brought me even closer to you.**"

Although *Glitter* had been a flop, Mariah kept trying. "One blip of a soundtrack does not ruin a life," she said. She worked on the movie *Wise Girls*, playing a waitress in a restaurant owned by the mob. Early reviewers raved about the movie. However, without a distributor it hit a dead end. Still, Mariah proved she

Mariah rocks at EuroBest in Paris, 2003. That year she continued to get back into the groove, winning a World Music Diamond Award in honor of over 100 million album sales worldwide. She also continued to support worthy causes that help children, especially the Make-A-Wish Foundation.

could act. The year 2003 ended on another high note, when Mariah received a World Music Award for selling more than 150 million albums.

REMEMBERING OTHERS

As Mariah struggled back to her feet, she continued to help others. She donated $100,000 to the Make-A-Wish Foundation, a group that grants wishes to children suffering from life-threatening illnesses. Many children wish to meet stars, like Mariah. She granted as many wishes as she could. She attended awards programs with children, took them to photo shoots, and met them backstage after concerts.

Making the World Better

Famous people often earn millions of dollars. With their fortune, many choose to help others who aren't so lucky. Celebrities often donate money and time to various charity groups. Because of their fame, they bring attention to good causes. Sometimes they even start charitable foundations themselves.

Often celebrities like Mariah pick charities that are important to them personally. Stars help with thousands of charities. They support finding cures for diseases, like AIDS and cancer, cleaning up the environment, protecting endangered animals, and helping children and families.

Mariah was inspired to help children with serious diseases and those living in inner-city neighborhoods because of her sister's actions. Since then, Mariah has helped bring change to people's lives. Mariah said, "I try to be a good person and make a difference where I can, in the world and with people."

In 2004, Mariah also volunteered to serve Thanksgiving dinner to poor families in New York City. She dished up turkey, stuffing, and vegetables. She also posed for pictures and chatted with kids and their families.

Despite her troubles, Mariah realized she was lucky. She also wanted to keep singing. And, she wanted to be back on top.

Chapter

5

❧ ✿ ❧

A MONSTER COMEBACK

MARIAH'S PAST FEW YEARS HAD BEEN VERY difficult. By 2005 she staged a comeback. In April, she released *The Emancipation of Mimi*, her 10th studio album. It quickly became the year's best-selling album. The song "We Belong Together" gave her another number-one hit, topping the charts for 14 weeks. Mariah was back.

Soon another one of her songs, "Don't Forget About Us," rose to the number-one spot. It was Mariah's 17th chart topper, and tied her with the King, Elvis Presley. Only The Beatles had more number-one singles. Mariah told reporters,

"I'm really fortunate, I'm really happy, and I'm really lucky to be where I am."

Mariah's powerful performance is a highlight of the evening as she sings her number-one hit "We Belong Together" at the 2005 BET Awards show. Her successful comeback began that year with her chart-topping album, *The Emancipation of Mimi*, which went multiplatinum.

Part of her new success came from collaborating with different artists. She had worked on the album with artists such as Jermaine Dupri, Kanye West, and Nelly. They helped give her latest album a new feel.

Working Together

African-American musician Jermaine Dupri does it all. He raps, writes, and produces. The Grammy-winning hip-hop artist has been in the music business from a young age. He performed as a dancer during Diana Ross's acts. At age 14, he produced his first record. In the early 1990s, he formed his own cutting-edge production company, So So Def. Today, Jermaine Dupri is the President of Urban Music at Virgin Records.

His debut album, *Jermaine Dupri Presents Life in 1472* went platinum. He has often collaborated with different artists, such as Usher, Twista, and Jay-Z. Jermaine and Mariah have produced several songs together.

In 1995, their song "Always Be My Baby" became Mariah's 11th number-one hit. Three years later the duo created "My All." They teamed up again for *The Emancipation of Mimi* album, combining their talents to create a stunning success.

MIMI'S RETURN

Mariah's family and close friends often call her Mimi, her inspiration for the name of her album. After her troubles of the past few years, Mariah was not afraid to be herself. She told *Parade* magazine,

> **"How do you climb back from the shambles when everybody counts you out? That can be a very a difficult thing to come to terms with, especially when you've had so much such success from such an early age. . . . More than anything, it was learning to grow up and take care of myself. Not treat myself like the corporation wanted to treat me, but treat myself like a human being. I've faced my worst fears and come out of them okay. Everything is always going to be all right as long as I hang in to the person inside of me."**

The *Emancipation of Mimi* went multiplatinum, becoming Mariah's most successful album in years. It proved to everyone that her career was not over. Once again, she was a megastar.

Mariah's new album captured several awards. She won three Grammys, one for best album, another for best song ("We Belong Together"), and the third for best performance. In addition, she won five Billboard Music Awards, four World Music Awards, and an NAACP Image Award.

Mariah can hardly hold all her trophies at the 2005 World Music Awards, where she won Best Selling R&B Artist, Best Selling Pop Female Artist, Female Entertainer of the Year, and Best Selling Single. She also won three Grammys and five Billboard Music Awards that year, proving she was a superstar once again.

DOING GOOD

That summer and fall, Mariah was busy. She, Jermaine Dupri, and Fat Man Scoop performed the opening number at the VH1 Save the Music Foundation benefit concert. She and other stars performed in Live 8 concerts around the world, encouraging wealthy nations to fight poverty in poorer countries. She also helped raise money for victims of Hurricane Katrina, a terrible storm that hit New Orleans, Louisiana. Viewers in at least 100 countries watched the televised concert. Stars like the Foo Fighters, Alicia Keys, Diddy, and U2 performed.

During the holidays, Mariah and the Fresh Air Fund served Thanksgiving dinner to people in need again, her annual tradition.

Mariah was excited about her upcoming tour in a 2006 appearance on *The Tonight Shown with Jay Leno*. The tour gave eager fans around the world a chance to see her live. A busy Mariah also worked on two movies, brought out her own perfume, and continued her work with charitable foundations.

She also continued her work with the Make-A-Wish Foundation. The group awarded her a Wish Icon Award to recognize the number of wishes she had granted and her dedication to their cause.

EXCITING TIMES

Mariah's fans wanted to see her live. Although Mariah still disliked touring, she started to plan the 2006 Adventures of Mimi Tour. She appeared on the popular *Tonight Show with Jay Leno* to talk about the upcoming tour and to perform her hit song "We Belong Together." Mariah's immense tour would take her to destinations in Africa, Canada, Asia, and throughout the United States. Although the tour was tiring and intense, Mariah was thrilled to be back. Her fans loved her.

Mariah still hadn't given up on her dream of acting. She began filming the *Tennessee*. In the film, she played Krystal, a woman who follows her dream to become a singer. Mariah composed the song "I've Got a Right to Dream," and sang it in the movie. Famous musician Willie Nelson played the guitar in the background. Soon Mariah began working on another movie, *Precious*, in which she played a social worker who helped teenagers.

Mariah also teamed up with a cosmetics company and released her own perfume called M. The scent was inspired by moments in Mariah's life. It hit the stores in 2007 and began selling quickly.

That fall, Mariah attended a huge gala for VH1's Save the Music Foundation. She and former president Bill Clinton were honored for their charity work. Their donations of time and money had helped provide musical instruments to schools across America. Mariah's interest showed how important music was to her. She told everyone,

> **"This is my love. I want to sing for the rest of my life."**

E=MC2

After her big comeback, Mariah attracted amazing amounts of media coverage. She was featured in newspapers, magazines, photographs, and advertisements around the world. She also

From Pop to Hip-hop

Mariah can sing the cool, slow blues and the hot, jumping dance hits. Her ability to combine different types of music thrills her fans. Blues, jazz, gospel, hip-hop, and pop, or popular music, are just a few kinds. Many of them have their roots in the African-American community.

Blues music is just that. Blue and sad. It originated with slaves who often sang to feel better as they worked in the fields. In the 1940s, blues music was combined with jazz, a swinging type of music made popular by African Americans. The jazz gave the blues a dance beat. The combination was called rhythm and blues or R&B music. It gave birth to rock and roll.

Gospel music originated in African-American churches in the United States. Its music, words, and sounds come from black ministers who wove their rhythmic preaching together with music from the choir. Singers like James Brown combined gospel and R&B to create emotionally-charged soul music.

Hip-hop started in the 1970s in New York City. It drew from dance club songs, street poetry, and other music. Rapping, or speaking rhyming words or poems to a beat, is a key ingredient of hip-hop.

began to appear on popular TV shows, talking about her upcoming album, *E=MC2*. She said, "It's like emancipation of Mariah Carey to the second power and beyond."

Mariah gave television viewers a taste of the new songs on the album. On the late-night television show *Saturday Night Live*, she performed "Touch My Body." Then, on *American Idol*, she sang "Bye Bye." She also served as a guest judge and helped coach new singers. On *American Idol Gives Back*, a charity telethon, she sang "Fly Like a Bird," with *American Idol* judge Randy Jackson playing backup for her on the bass guitar.

On April 15, 2008, *E=MC2* hit the stores. The album was a huge success. The song "Touch My Body" became her 18th number-one single. She now had more hits than Elvis Presley. Only The Beatles, with 20 number-one hits, had more. She said,

> "When I have a minute to reflect, I realize my life has been pretty amazing. But I consider myself a normal person who wants a normal life. It's exciting to do what I do, but I also like to stay real and grounded."

TRUE LOVE

Mariah's personal life, too, was a success. While taping her latest video, she had met actor Nick Cannon. The two found they had much in common and began dating. They quickly fell in love. "I never felt a love like this was in the cards for me," Mariah said.

A relaxed Mariah promotes her new album *E=MC2* in a 2008 performance on *Saturday Night Live*. Mariah made many television appearances to support the record, which included the hit song, "Touch My Body." Her 18th number-one single broke the record previously held by Elvis Presley.

MAY 19, 2008

People

FASHION'S BIG NIGHT
INSIDE THE MOST GLAMOROUS PARTY OF THE YEAR

EXCLUSIVE PHOTOS!

MARIAHDAILY.COM

MARIAH'S SECRET WEDDING!

The singer and new husband Nick Cannon share the details of their six-week romance and surprise wedding

BRITNEY'S VICTORY
WINS MORE TIME WITH HER BOYS

$3.99US $4.79CAN

0 92567 10227 3

PEOPLE.COM

Mariah's personal life was the delight of the news media. Her wedding to Nick Cannon received coverage all over the world in 2008. But even getting married didn't change Mariah's focus on her work, as she started working on a new album and brought out a second perfume.

On April 30, 2008, Mariah and Nick Cannon married at her estate in the Bahamas. Their wedding was quiet and small, with only 12 guests. As the sun set, they dined on lobster and drank champagne.

Mariah's marriage didn't slow her work, though. She was already planning another album. She also released a second perfume, called Luscious Pink, which she said smelled like warm, velvety-soft flowers.

THE AMERICAN DREAM

In November 2008, Americans elected a new president, Barack Obama. Like Mariah, Obama is biracial. After many years of racial discrimination, it was an amazing achievement for the country. Mariah received a huge honor when she was asked to attend a ball after the new president's **inauguration** in January 2009.

President Obama had planned the Neighborhood Inaugural Ball to celebrate the day he became president. The ball was held in a large convention center in Washington D.C. Many celebrities performed for the attendees and the millions of people watching on TV. Musicians Beyoncé, Jay-Z, Alicia Keys, Sting, and others performed. Famous actors like Leonardo DiCaprio and Jamie Foxx also appeared on stage.

Mariah was one of the highlights of the ball. She sang the inspirational song "Hero" from her 1994 album. She said proudly,

"I wrote this song to inspire people that anything is possible. Tonight I think we believe that, a whole lot more. This is for everybody out there with a dream, and of course, I have to dedicate it to our new president."

AN AMAZING CAREER

Mariah has been singing for nearly 20 years, winning many of music's most prestigious awards. She had snapped up numerous Grammy, American Music, World Music, and Billboard Awards. She has also received recognition for her generous charity work.

Mariah was inspired by the election of Barack Obama as she performed her song, "Hero," during an inaugural ball in Washington D.C. in 2009. Mariah also has been an inspiration. Her talent, record-setting hits, and commitment to helping others continue to show young people that they, too, can fulfill their dreams.

Going to the Ball

The day a new president is sworn in, there is a big ceremony and a long parade. That night, fireworks light the sky and people attend inaugural balls, or parties, across Washington D.C. Often, the people who attend helped the new president win the election. The president and first lady stop by each ball for a short time. They dance and thank people for their support. It's the highlight of the ball.

Long ago, wealthy guests arrived at inaugural balls in horse-drawn coaches. They dined on delicacies like oysters and fine cheeses. By 2005, inaugural balls had changed. Tickets went for $150 each. Guests munched on free cookies and bought bottles of water.

President Barack Obama's Neighborhood Inaugural Ball was quite different. He didn't want a glitzy, black-tie occasion just for the wealthy people who contributed to his campaign. He wanted it to be open to everyday people, along with his campaign workers, family, and friends. The ball was aired on TV stations across the nation, so that more people could "attend" by watching. Mariah and other stars helped celebrate the big occasion.

Mariah has set many new records. She is the only artist to have her first five singles top the charts. She also has spent more time at the number-one spot on the charts than anyone else. With 18 number-one singles, Mariah has more chart-topping hits than any solo artist in the United States. She stands second overall only to The Beatles. If her latest album, $E=MC2$, indicates her future success, she could easily bypass The Beatles' record. She hopes to keep singing for many years to come, and shows no signs of slowing.

Mariah's sensational achievements are especially amazing considering her difficult childhood. Being raised in a rough neighborhood by a single parent wasn't easy. She faced harsh discrimination for being biracial. She held onto her dream, though, and overcame tough times. Mariah tells everyone,

"I want to encourage anyone else out there who feels like maybe they can't overcome an obstacle. I feel like I'm living proof . . . never lose your faith."

1970   Mariah Carey is born to Alfred, an African American and Venezuelan, and Patricia, of Irish descent, on March 27 in Long Island, New York.

1973   Mariah's parents divorce.

1974   Mariah's mother begins giving her voice lessons.

1987   Graduates from high school and moves to Manhattan.

1988   Meets Sony Music executive Tommy Mottola and signs her first contract.

1990   Releases *Mariah Carey*, her debut album.

      "Vision of Love" and "Love Takes Time" become number-one hits.

1991   Wins two Grammy Awards.

      Releases *Emotions*.

      Becomes the only artist to have her first five singles top the charts.

1992   Releases *Mariah Carey: MTV Unplugged*, donates proceeds to charity.

1993   Marries Tommy Mottola.

      Releases *Music Box*.

1994   Founds Camp Mariah with the Fresh Air Fund.

      Releases *Merry Christmas*.

1995   Releases *Daydream*.

1996   Leaves Tommy Mottola and soon divorces.

1997   Changes her image and singing style.

      Releases *Butterfly*.

1998   Begins working with the National Adoption Center.

1999   Releases *Rainbow*.

      Receives the Congressional Award for her charity work.

2000   Receives the Female Artist of the Millennium award.

      Becomes the Make-A-Wish Celebrity Wish Granter of the Year.

2001   Checks into a psychiatric hospital.

2002   Releases *Charmbracelet*.

2004   Serves Thanksgiving dinner with the Fresh Air Fund.

2005   Releases *The Emancipation of Mimi*.

Ties Elvis Presley for most number-one hits by a solo artist.

2006   Wins three Grammy Awards.

2007   Receives honors from the Save the Music Foundation for volunteer work.

2008   Releases *E=MC2*.

With her 18th number-one hit, becomes the solo artist in the U.S. with the most chart-topping singles.

Marries Nick Cannon.

2009   Performs at President Barack Obama's Neighborhood Inaugural Ball.

Albums

1990	*Mariah Carey*
1991	*Emotions*
1992	*MTV Unplugged*
1993	*Music Box*
1994	*Merry Christmas*
1995	*Daydream*
1997	*Butterfly*
1998	*#1s*
1999	*Rainbow*
2001	*Glitter*
	Greatest Hits
2002	*Charmbracelet*
2003	*The Remixes*
2005	*The Emancipation of Mimi*
2008	*E=MC2*

Number-one Singles

1990	"Vision of Love"
	"Love Takes Time"
1991	"Someday"
	"I Don't Wanna Cry"
	"Emotions"
1992	"I'll Be There"
1993	"Dreamlover"
	"Hero"
1995	"Fantasy"
	"One Sweet Day" (with Boyz II Men)
1996	"Always Be My Baby"
1997	"Honey"
1998	"My All"
1999	"Heartbreaker" (with Jay-Z)
	"Thank God I Found You" (with Joe and 98 Degrees)
2005	"We Belong Together"
	"Don't Forget About Us"
2008	"Touch My Body"

Filmography

1999	*The Bachelor*
2001	*Glittler*
2002	*WiseGirls*
2003	*Death of a Dynasty*
2005	*State Property 2*
2008	*You Don't Mess with the Zohan* (cameo appearance)
2009	*Tennessee* (to be released in June 2009)
2009	*Precious* (to be released in November 2009)

Selected Awards

1991   American Music Award; BMI Award; Grammy Awards; Soul Train Awards

1992   American Music Award; Billboard Music Awards; BMI Award

1993   American Music Awards

1994   ARIA Awards; Billboard Award; *Bravo* Magazine Award

1995   American Music Award; Blockbuster Award; World Music Awards

1996   American Music Awards; Billboard Music Awards; BMI Award; Blockbuster Awards; National Dance Music Awards; World Music Awards

1998   American Music Award; Billboard Music Awards; Blockbuster Awards; BMI Award; Soul Train Lady of Soul Award; World Music Awards

1999   Billboard Music Award; Blockbuster Award; BMI Award; NAACP Image Award; Oscar Academy Award; The Congressional Award

2000   American Music Award; Blockbuster Award; VH1 Award; World Music Awards

2001   Make-A-Wish Foundation's 2000 Chris Greicius Award; Radio Music Award

2003   Fresh Air Fund American Heroes Award; Soul Train Award; World Music Award

2005   American Music Award; Billboard Awards; Radio Music Awards; Soul Train Lady of Soul Awards; Teen Choice Awards; World Music Awards

2006   Billboard Awards; BMI Awards; Grammy Awards; NAACP Image Award; Make-A-Wish Foundation's Wish Icon Award; Soul Train Awards

2007   BMI Award; Hollywood Walk of Fame Award; VH1 Award

2008   American Music Award; MTV Japan Video Music Award; World Music Award

AIDS—a deadly disease caused by a virus that attacks a person's ability to fight germs.

ballads—slow love songs.

civil rights movement—a long struggle in the 1950s and 1960s that ended the unfair laws and customs that prevented black Americans from having same rights as whites.

debut—the first performance.

gospel—emotional religious music that began in African-American churches in the U.S.

Grammy Award—an annual award presented by the National Academy of Recording Arts & Sciences to honor outstanding musicians.

hip-hop—a mix of different kinds of music with pounding rhythms and rap, started in the 1970s by inner-city African-American teens.

inauguration—a formal ceremony when a new president takes office.

platinum—when an album sells one million copies, or a single sells two million copies.

racism—treating people unfairly because of the color of their skin.

R&B—rhythm and blues, a combination of blues and jazz that started rock and roll.

range—the distance between the lowest and highest note a voice or instrument can hit.

singles—individual songs from an album.

soul—a type of music with catchy rhythms that combines R&B and gospel.

Books

Kandel, Bethany. *Growing Up Biracial: Trevor's Story*. Minneapolis, MN: Lerner Publications, 1997.

Scott, Cecilia. *Mariah Carey*. Broomall, PA: Mason Crest Publishers, 2007.

Shapiro, Marc. *Mariah Carey*. Toronto, Ontario: ECW Press, 2001.

Waters, Rosa. *Hip-Hop: A Short History*. Broomall, PA: Mason Crest Publishers, 2007.

Periodicals

Hoffman, Melody K. "Mariah Carey: On Her Past, Present, and Future in Music." *Jet* (April 25, 2005).

Kaplan, James. "I've Faced My Worst Fears." *Parade Magazine* (February 24, 2008): http://www.parade.com.

Norent, Lynn. "Mariah Carey: 'Not Just Another White Girl Trying to Sing Black.'" *Ebony* (March 1, 1991).

Ogunnaike, Lola. "A Superstar Returns with Another New Self." *The New York Times* (April 12, 2005): http://www.nytimes.com.

Web Sites

www.exploratorium.edu/music/
The Exploratorium's Science of Music site offers interactive games to experiment with mixing sounds, rhythms, and styles, along with facts about different types of music.

www.freshair.org
The Fresh Air Fund's site gives information about the charity and Camp Mariah.

www.mariahcarey.com
Mariah Carey's official Web site contains news about Mariah, photos, her career accomplishments, links to the causes she supports, and a forum for her fans.

www.mcarchives.com
The Mariah Carey Archives provides news and a detailed biography of Mariah's life.

www.wish.org
The Make-A-Wish Foundation's site tells more about the top wish-granting charity for children who face life-threatening illnesses.

PICTURE CREDITS

ABOUT THE AUTHOR

Kerrily Sapet has written numerous books and magazine articles for children. This book took her on a musical journey—from mournful soul to pounding hip-hop. She lives in Chicago, Illinois with her husband, Jason, her son, Ben, and her crazy yellow dog, Tess.